"The Early Years of McFarlane Toys: The Action Behind the Figures"

By Paul Burke

with Bill Martin, Anthony Billotto,

Rick Privman, and Stephen T. Gouge

Foreword by Alan Hassenfeld

Design, Layout, Cover, and Editing by
Stephen T. Gouge

The Early Years of McFarlane Toys - The Action Behind the Figures™. Published by Asylum Publications, Inc. Distributed by Binary Publications. All photos and artwork are copyright © by their respective owners. Asylum™ and the logo are TM 2019. All rights reserved. Including the right to reproduce this book or portions thereof in any form, except in the context of a brief review.

ISBN: 978-1-7339309-1-8

1 3 5 7 9 10 8 6 4 2

If you are interested in obtaining more information regarding Asylum Publications, custom photo/art books or wholesale opportunities. Please contact us at asylumpublications75@gmail.com.

Dedication

This book is dedicated to all of the employees, contractors, suppliers to all of the McFarlane companies, the fans, and of course, Todd McFarlane, whose creative vision and dedication to producing great products and publications made this journey possible.

Foreword

McFarlane Toys came on the market in 1994 with a bang. Their idea of large, complex, highly decorated action figures added a new category, Ultra Action Figures, to the marketplace. It was an exciting time for the industry and the folks at McFarlane led the way with action figure designs raising the bar for excellence each year.

As McFarlane Toys matured, their non-traditional promotion efforts raised the company to new heights in popularity every year. Their New York showroom became a "must see" for everyone in the industry as they built out themed, dedicated rooms for each line of toys setting a standard in the industry that we all strived to meet.

It was a pleasure watching the company grow and prosper. I and the Hasbro team were proud to call the management team at McFarlane friends.

Alan Hassenfeld
Former Chairman and CEO of Hasbro Toys

We got by with a little help from our friends.

1994-2000

PLYMOUTH
Paul Burke
Gary Reed
William Martin
Bob LoMonaco
Eric Light
Vern Mitchell
Rick Beer
Allan Inglis
Patrick Carron
Beth Vaisanen-Sullivan
Jennifer Pankowski
Danielle Ditzek Spears
Bambi Fisher
Matt Hamilton
Bob Vogt
Jason McFarlane
Lise McFarlane
Bob McFarlane
Terry Lewis
Chuck Yates
Scott Martyniuk
Redd Lynch
Aaron Gelman
Richard Jorgensen
Chet Jacques
Beau Smith
Brian Erickson
Tina DiCicco
Jon Chick
Eric Topliss
Doug Hartley
Jim Hedstrom
Christina Rincon
Ed LoMonaco
Tina Daniels
Ian Cooper
Dan Wilson
Mary Kwilos

Jeff Burke
Mike Vescoso
Dave Eisenhardt

HONG KONG
Victor Wong

NEW JERSEY DESIGN
Anthony Billotto
Edward Frank
Andy Frank
Eric Treadway
Jim Preziosi
Kathy Faline
Billy Mancuso
Eric "Cornboy" Mayse
Derrick Miller
Christopher Dahlberg
Steve "The Victim" Hamady
Jean St. Jean
Oliver Brig

SHOWROOM CONTRACTORS
Ken Hoare
Carmelo "Snow" Sigona
William Shopland
Dan Marchese
James Byrne, Jr.
Tom Taggert

STABUR / CALIBER
Nancy Durand
Nathan Pride
Jim Pruett
Joe Pruett
Gretchen Burke
Tim Parsons
Joe Martin

PHOENIX
Todd McFarlane
Terence "Terry" Fitzgerald
Wanda Kolomyjec
Al Simmons
Julia Simmons
Sheila Egger
Tiffany McFarlane
Carmen Bryant
Melanie Simmons
Sheri Halvorson
Joseph Ferstl
Drew Hutchinson
Eric Orlaska

OTHERS
Rick Privman
Yumiko Miyano
George Irwin
Peter Irwin
Norman Meyers
Bob Mendelo
Mike (Irwin sales)
Ed Nakano
Kevin Sweet
Al Gilly
Loren Taylor
Harold Anderson
Byron Wilkes
Charles Ip
Frankie Yeh
Danny To
Bobby Chen
Bob Juranich

Apologies for those that we may have missed as there were so many talented people that had a part in it all.

I had been working with Stabur / Caliber Comics on a few Spawn projects in 1992 and 1993. Todd McFarlane became a personal friend during the production of "The Comic Book Greats" video series.

The Comic Book Greats was a video series produced by Paul Burke, starring Stan Lee, and featured some of the greatest individuals in comic books.

SPAWN MOBILE

One of the first promotional items Todd created was the Spawn Mobile. The Spawn Mobile was a real "funny car," with artwork designed by Todd, Terry Fitzgerald and Chance Wolf, one of Todd's early creative staff members. Al Simmons used to tour the country at conventions and events in costume as the Spawn character along with the Spawn Mobile.

The first toy that Todd produced was a Hot Wheels Spawn Mobile used for promotion.

One of the many Al Simmons stories that stands out in my mind is when I received a call from Al one day. He was at Seattle's SEATAC airport getting ready to fly back to Phoenix on a break. Al asked if anyone had called the office regarding the car trailer and I said we haven't heard from anyone. Apparently, Al was driving on Interstate 5 and people would pull up next to him and wave. This wasn't uncommon as people always waved at the Spawn trucks. But when he parked at the airport parking lot, he noticed that the roof of the car trailer had pulled away and pealed back, throwing the majority of the roof and its air conditioner onto the freeway. We never received any complaints. We just replaced the trailer.

Our custom '55 Chevy, dubbed "The Crime Mobile," from the Sam & Twitch comic was also brought to life and later toured with the Spawn Mobile to conventions.

Two different versions of the single carded Spawn Mobile were released. One with bats on the hood and one without.

Todd had wanted to manufacture 50,000 Spawn Mobile Hot Wheel cars for promotion, but Mattel required a minimum purchase of 100,000 units. So Todd sold the other 50,000 cars at his cost to ANCO, a contract "leased space" supplier to Walmart. I had already been selling Disney and Caliber comic books, and Todd his Spawn comic books, to Walmart thru ANCO. ANCO bundled the Spawn Mobile Hot Wheels with a comic book and placed them in Walmart bundled for a retail price of $9.95. At the time, a regular Hot Wheel car normally sold for only 88 cents each at retail.

Shortly thereafter, in early November 1993, Todd paged me as I was driving home from New York. I stopped at a Dunkin Donuts in Ledgewood, New Jersey and called him from a pay phone. Todd was upset with Mattel because they wanted to license Spawn for action figures and toys, but would not allow him any creative control. We talked about Stabur producing an action figure for Spawn and Todd said "If you can get Walmart to buy toys, we'll make them."

As he was saying this, I was paged by Harold Anderson of ANCO Treat, a contract "leased space" supplier to Walmart. I told Todd I would call him back. I called Harold and Harold said he needed Spawn toys ASAP. Walmart had sold out of their 50,000 Spawn Mobiles in 30 days.

I told Harold what was happening and that we'd agree to make toys. I called Todd back and gave him the good news about ANCO Treat. Our world had changed in the course of 15 minutes and the rest is history.

It was a hot bed of activity for this small group creating and publishing the #1 comic book every month, then reviewing and contemplating numerous worldwide licensing in and out deals and entertainment deals. At the same time, Todd and Terry created innovative and unique promotion to build the property and make Spawn a household name.

Todd lived in West Lynn, Oregon, just outside of Portland in the early 90's. This is where Spawn the comic book began and all production took place until 1994. The studio office was on the top floor of his house and featured two desks, a fax machine and a lime green velvet couch. Terry Fitzgerald joined Todd in 1992 to assist in publishing, writing, illustration, licensing, entertainment and overall management, including management of Todd's portion of Image Comics. They were hoping to sell 75-100,000 copies of issue number one of Spawn and instead sold over one million. The first year's sales topped 13 million comics because of the dedication of Todd to get each issue out on time every month.

Well over four months were spent negotiating with Mattel for a toy license, only for them to pull the rug out from under them after the Last Action Hero movie tanked at the box office. Terry had negotiated a six figure deal with a nice royalty rate, but after the poor performance of the movie, Mattel changed their terms to less than 10% of what was previously offered. The gents were not happy. They decided that if they were dumb enough to start a comic book company and take on a hundred million dollar company like Marvel or DC, why not be really stupid and start a toy company and take on a billion dollar company like Mattel or Hasbro? They reached out to Paul Burke at Stabur and McFarlane Toys was born.

Interestingly enough, the company's original name was Todd Toys, but after a cease and desist letter from Mattel (who owned the trademark "Todd," a Barbie / McDonald's Happy Meal character), the name was changed to McFarlane Toys. Shortly thereafter Julia Simmons joined the Portland team and took over the office management duties.

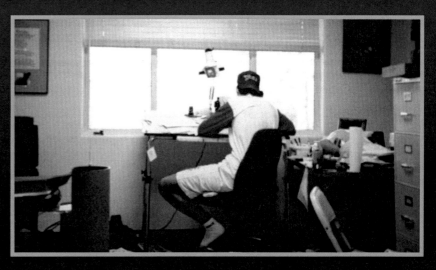

STABUR CORPORATION

The Stabur Corporation / Caliber Comics was a small company with eight employees managed by Paul Burke, Gary Reed, Bill Martin, and other independent partners. The company was known for publishing numerous independent comic books on a monthly basis, publishing trade books, being the leading print publisher for syndicate cartoonists, producing The Comic Book Greats video series with Stan Lee, and manufacturing hundreds of other products for the collector market.

It was the "go-to" company for special projects. From MAD Magazine, Rocky Horror Anniversary Events, Penthouse, Theme Park Magazine, 20th Century Fox, Gemstone Marketing (jewelry) and on.

It was a dynamic company, known for fast turnaround of "high quality" product that always had something new on the development plate.

Working with Todd on a toy company brought an excitement and a work demand that we couldn't imagine. We had to add a toy design team and specialists in toy marketing right away. After a few meetings and an interview with Todd, we brought Tony Billotto and Ed Frank on board to the Todd McFarlane Productions team to head up the McFarlane Design Group in New Jersey and to design action figures for TMP Toys (the first company name).

We then brought Andy Frank, one of our graphic artists, on board full time and added Loren Taylor to assist in developing the toy company with Bob LoMonaco as the Vice President of Sales, both experienced toy executives.

The combination of people from Portland, Detroit, and New Jersey created the company and first toy line in 60 days for our first appearance at New York Toy Fair in February, 1994.

As a joke, the first design Tony and Ed faxed over was "Violator Cow" for a Spawn Barnyard Series. I envisioned my career being over in an instant. But it would have been a great line of toys.

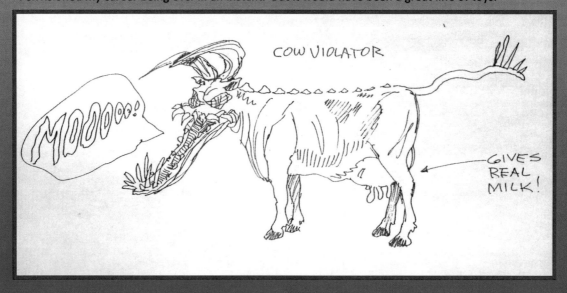

In 1994, Stabur published the pictorial biography of Fabio, the popular male model who appeared on romance novel covers. Stabur also produced numerous Fabio products for a Fabio QVC program. All of the new hires at McFarlane Toys in Plymouth, Michigan were given a Fabio book, a couple of t-shirts with Fabio's image and a case of four Fabio throw pillows. They were required to wear a Fabio t-shirt during their first week of employment.

Bill Shopland

Ed Frank and Kathy Faline review reference material.

Even Spawn is not exempt from meeting sculpting deadlines.

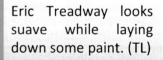

Eric Treadway looks suave while laying down some paint. (TL)

Ed Frank adds some final touches to a Spawn sculpt. (TR)

Jim Preziosi (ML)

Derrick Miller works on paint apps. (BL)

1994 TOY FAIR & PROMOTION

The two month rush to get a toys designed, prototyped and a presentation for the 1994 New York Toy Fair was quite an achievement for the TMP team. We had a small area in the Al Gilly Showroom with a few prototypes and clamshells with boarded paintings of the toys to demonstrate how they would look on the shelf. Considering the time we had to prepare, we did a good job and got a great reception from the buyers. The press for the toy magazines understood what we were doing and the coverage from Lee's Toy and Action Figure Review and other publications created a demand from consumers that generated sales that surpassed our 1994 goals.

Interestingly, we were listed as TMP Toys during this period and shortly thereafter changed the toy company name to Todd Toys.

SPAWN SERIES 1

Overkill

This massive villain was comic book born. His head shot out for extreme head butting action. He carried a bent parking meter as a club. During production, the factory "forgot" to make the spray masks for the meter that would have indicated the price for parking, so they wrote "5¢" with a marker! This embarrassing faux pas caused Todd much consternation. The factory quickly corrected the mistake. Ironically, the "magic marker 5 cent Overkill" became one of the most sought after collector figures.

Spawn

Our #1 figure was based on Todd's incredibly successful comic book creation. This character drove everything that McFarlane Toys made. This award winning Spawn figure came with a huge flexible cape that could be posed to wrap his body or fly open. He carried a two-by-four with a spike to smash his foes. The waist chains could be removed to be used as weapons. A scarred and burned Al Simmons head was also produced to create a collector variation.

Clown

The first Clown figure was based on the comic book representation. It had two heads, the Clown's real head and a Clown demon head that rotated out of the body. The comedic touch was a large handheld turkey drumstick with a bite taken out of it.

Medieval Spawn

Based on the comic book character, this figure had a removable plastic cape, a large hand held sword, a spinning shield with blades and removable waist chains that could be used a weapon.

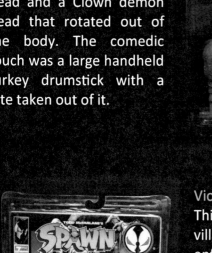

Violator

This comic book based villain was Malebolgia's enforcer. Todd wanted him to be produced as a bendy so that he could be easily posed in radically animated positions and be a creative alternative to conventionally articulated figures. By moving the huge horn back and forth, the Violator could use his fang filled jaw to "bite" other figures!

Tremor

This chunky demon dude was built for power. He had a spring loaded bionic left arm that could knock any figure off it's feet.

Spawn Alley Playset

This was a large put-together play environment. Spawn Alley was sized in scale with our figures and vehicles. Play actions included an exploding brick wall, an avalanche roof, a missile firing gun, a booby trap manhole cover with a trash can, a secret Spawn Mobile garage, a working crane with hook and cable, a telephone pole swing, an elevator, a loading dock, two rats and one vulture. Todd loved the fact that we included rats. Play pieces like that never came with a Barbie Dream House!

Spawn Mobile

Spawn needed cool wheels so we gave him the Spawn Mobile. This cross between a muscle car and a dragster had a pop-up engine equipped with a pop-out Gatling gun. The spring loaded spoiler launched a "metal" skull and chains. Secret side panels popped open to launch hidden missiles. Chain-covered racing slicks, a battering ram bumper, a tow winch, and wheelie bars added more style and play value.

Violator Monster Rig

Spawn had his Spawn Mobile, so Violator had his evil big rig which combined organic and mechanical styling. The removable roof panel allowed the bendy Violator figure to ride inside. The lower spike-toothed jaw could bite foes when the spoiler was pushed down. Two spikes could be launched from each side and there was a tow hitch in the back. The bone cage could be removed to imprison captured enemies. Heavy duty rolling truck wheels completed this ultra vehicle.

Todd and TMP produced three large budget, professional television commercials that aired in 1994 and 1995 for the United States. The major retailers would request commercials to drive toy sales and we produced the commercials to satisfy them. Each commercial was broadcast in major cities for a short period of time and we stopped each advertising program after a week or two. Our action figures would sell out at the stores before the commercials would air. The company and Irwin Toys also produced a number of low budget television commercials for broadcast in Canada. These commercials would broadcast on regional television stations and drive sales locally.

One of the many challenges of that shoot was to create a Gatling gun for the hood of the real car. Loren Taylor, my son Christian and I ran out to Toys R Us and a hardware store to buy parts. That night I adapted a toy Gatling gun, using some PVC pipe fittings and odds and ends that I "found" at the film studio. Some spray paint, duct tape and a ton of hot glue completed the prop. Bill Shopland rigged up some very tricky exploding effects for the Spawn Alley Playset. This was just more adventure that would never have happened if not for Todd wanting to make toys.

-Tony B.

SPAWN
We're out to blast the competition.

1994 FACTORY

After reviewing a number of factories in China, we selected APEX Manufacturing, owned by Bobby Chen and Danny To, to be our primary factory in 1994.

The toy parts were injection molded and airbrushed using paint masks. Then all of the detail was hand-painted by very skilled employees. Note the one young lady (above) painting Spawn's face holding four brushes in her hand!

Each toy was hand assembled using a simple conveyor with each employee adding a single part to the toy.

SPAWN POWER CARDZ

Spawn Power Cardz were developed by Gary Reed, Joe Martin and Tim Parsons for Caliber Game Systems (Caliber Comics) in 1994 as one of the first licensed products from Todd McFarlane Productions. It took over one year of product design and development with both Todd and Gary perfecting the look and play of the game. Thousands of game cards were produced and released through a number of comic book and game distributors.

However, the printers' salesman / job coordinator had neglected to collate 95% of the trading cards, causing single boxes to have only one or two different cards in each deck. This resulted in most of them being returned to Caliber. The playing cards were then sent back the printer to be destroyed. This makes complete sets of the cards hard to piece together.

In the summer of 1994, Todd McFarlane Productions purchased its first cargo van for conventions and promotion. In true TMP fashion, we just couldn't decal our vehicles. We had Terry Large, a mural artist from Stadium Services / Apex, airbrush paint the van with Spawn and our logos in one of our warehouses.

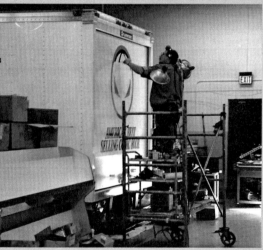

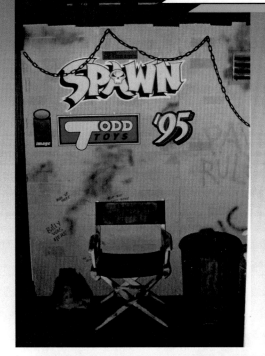

Our strong toy sales in 1994 gave the company a lot of attention going into the New Year.

In 1995 we were able to expand our exhibit space in Al Gilly's showroom for the '95 New York Toy Fair. We had a larger, main exhibit room, a conference area, and a shared reception room.

The 1995 toy lines consisted of Spawn Series #2 and Series #3 and extended out
to include a Youngblood and Wetworks line of action figures from Image Comics.

The sales success of the 1995 Toy Fair established Todd Toys as a company with a future.

TODD TOYS™

SPAWN WETWORKS YOUNGBLOOD

SPAWN

Based on the number ONE comic for the last three years!!!

Figure Assortment:
• Spawn (new)
• Vaporizer
• The Curse
• Violator (new)
• Cosmic Angela
• The Redeemer
• Ninja Spawn

Available 8/95

Item # 10120
Dimensions- 13 x 7¹/₈ x 4¹/₂
Carton Pack (12)
Carton weight- 9.0
Carton cube- 2.52
Carton Dimensions- 22¹/₂ x 12¹/₂ x 15¹/₂

FALL

YOUNGBLOOD™

The largest selling family of the superhot Image Comics!

Figure Assortment:
• Troll
• Dutch
• Die-Hard
• Shaft
• Crypt
• Sentinel

Available 8/95

Item # 12100
Dimensions- 13 x 7¹/₈ x 4¹/₂
Carton Pack (12)
Carton weight- 9.0
Carton cube- 2.52
Carton Dimensions- 22¹/₂ x 12¹/₂ x 15¹/₂

1995

WETWORKS™

Based on the military action title that debuted at the top of the charts!

Figure Assortment:
• Dane
• Dozer
• Mother-1
• Vampire
• Werewolf
• Grail

Available 8/95

Item # 13100
Dimensions- 13 x 7¹/₈ x 4¹/₂
Carton Pack (12)
Carton weight- 9.0
Carton cube- 2.52
Carton Dimensions- 22¹/₂ x 12¹/₂ x 15¹/₂

TODD TOYS™

1995 was a pivotal year for Todd McFarlane Productions. The McFarlane Design Group team moved into a small office and warehouse to accommodate the ever expanding equipment and design crew. The Detroit office expanded its offices and warehouse area and TMP opened an office in Tempe to handle the growing staff in Arizona. The company changed its name from Todd Toys to McFarlane Toys. We created our first subsidiary McFarlane Toys Asia in Hong Kong to handle all of our manufacturing and McFarlane Toys Canada, Inc. for all Canadian sales made through our Canadian distributors Irwin Toys.

Irwin Toys had planned a Spawn slot car racetrack called Spawn Battle Terror. The slot cars were to be versions of the Spawn Mobile and Violator Monster Rig. Sadly, it never went beyond the mock up stage of production.

As we move through the figures and vehicles, it's easy to see that every new line was better than the previous line. As we became more confident, the detail, poses, accessories, and decoration became more and more complex.

It is important to note that McFarlane Toys was the first toy company to make action figures more realistic, more human, more detailed, and with a much higher level of decoration. Todd simply asked the question, "Why don't toy companies make more realistic figures?" My answer was, "Molding is molding. There really is no technical reason for not making figures look real. It just comes down to styling and sculpting."

It is also easy to see that we evolved from making "toy toys" to making "collector toys." No other toy company, at that time, made "collector toys." All toy companies were making toys for children to play with. If someone came along and decided to collect those regular toys after the fact, that was OK, but the toys were not made to be collected. The Spawn Alley Playset, the Battle Horse, Spawn Mobile, etc. were TOYS in the true sense of being toys. They were cool toys, but they were toys, which is what Ed and I had been designing for years. It was Todd who realized that we could make toys with the sole purpose of being collected.

We started getting feedback from the fans of Image Comics that they were buying at least two of each of our figures. One to open and "play with" and one to archive. The light went off in our heads and we were off to the races making collector figures.

Also, neither Ed Frank nor I had ever designed action figures. We designed and invented lots of pre-school toys, ride-on toys, sand toys, games, sporting goods, dolls, construction toys, etc., but no action figures. It was amazing that Todd, a comic book artist whose style I was familiar with, gave us a shot. Todd and Paul really took a chance with us.

-Tony Billotto

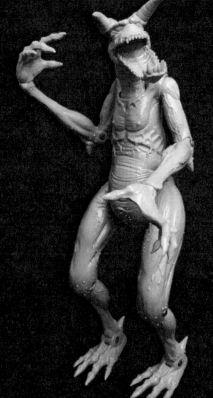

Malebolgia test shot prototype.

Malebolgia hand painted paint sample.

Malebolgia in package. Original paint scheme.

Malebolgia figure repaint
with purple and teal highlights.

We had to package Malebolgia in a crunched up crouching pose so that the figure could be packed out in the same assortment. It was an expensive figure to produce because it was at least twice the size of the other figures. Even so, we (Todd) kept the price at the same level as the other figures. When I told Todd that we would not make money on that figure, he said that he was "making it scale for the fans." That consideration went a long way and helped to cement his great relationship with Spawn and McFarlane collectors.

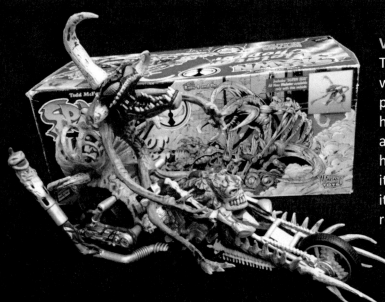

Violator Chopper

The Violator and the Air Cycle were more affordable lower-priced vehicles. The Chopper was highly decorated and difficult to assemble at the factory. The handlebars were articulated and it had a massive rear slick to help it balance. Bendy Violator was resized larger to fit the Chopper.

Spawn Air Cycle

This was a companion piece for Pilot Spawn who could slip into the cockpit by removing his jet pack. It had a flying Spawn cape, firing missiles, landing skids, twin engines and a handlebar/windshield assembly.

Battle Horse

Spawn had his hot rod and Medieval Spawn had his Battle Horse. This formidable beast had a spring loaded catapult that could fling a boulder, a huge jousting lance, a hand held mace and chain, battle axe and articulated legs. The Battle Horse was very popular toy and prized by collectors.

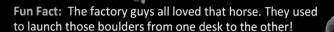

Fun Fact: The factory guys all loved that horse. They used to launch those boulders from one desk to the other!

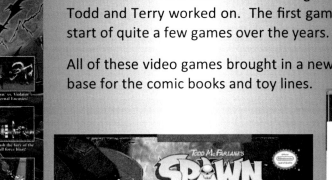

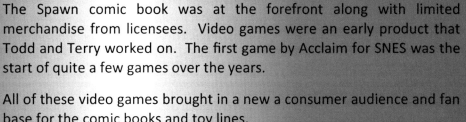

In the early days, the popularity of Spawn came from numerous areas. The Spawn comic book was at the forefront along with limited merchandise from licensees. Video games were an early product that Todd and Terry worked on. The first game by Acclaim for SNES was the start of quite a few games over the years.

All of these video games brought in a new a consumer audience and fan base for the comic books and toy lines.

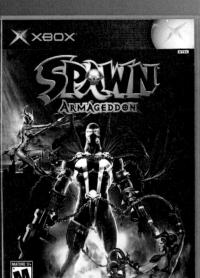

YOUTH HOCKEY

Stabur / Caliber had been sponsoring youth hockey teams for children twelve years old and younger. After we produced the Comic Book Greats Video Series together, Todd McFarlane became a sponsor and we started promoting Spawn with youth hockey teams.

We eventually moved up to promoting talented young players on two travel Spawn teams that played against some of the best teams in the US and Canada. Our home ice in Plymouth, Michigan was the home of the Plymouth Whalers, a Major Junior professional hockey team.

Todd McFarlane Productions was a heavy sponsor of the arena with signage and its own custom painted Zamboni that turned colors, from black to purple to gold as it reflected under the arena lighting. The Zamboni was exhibited in Las Vegas for a hockey equipment convention.

TMP sponsored a youth hockey team of boys aged nine to twelve from Russia to play US teams in the Midwest. It was a thrill for us to have them and of course, the team had a great time and went home with equipment, toys, comic books and more.

The Spawn hockey jerseys were very popular. Fans continually tried to purchase player's jerseys for hundreds of dollars and a few times we told the kids to sell the jersey after the game, we would replace it. One of the highlights of the jerseys was that the Detroit Red Wings (NHL) used to wear the Spawn practice jerseys during their practices.

The last year of sponsorship was in 1999. The Spawn Double A Bantam team won the 1999 Michigan State Championship and was a runner-up in the National Finals in St. Louis.

TMP's love for hockey evolved into a small partial ownership of the Edmonton Oilers NHL team through McFarlane Toys Canada.

1995 FACTORY

The company continued to expand with additional factories in 1995 to manufacture the various action figure lines and playsets. Our new subsidiary, TMP Asia, was established to guarantee the quality and make the tooling the company required to produce the highest quality toys possible.

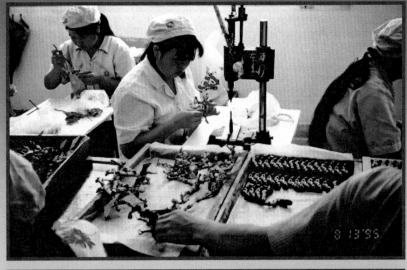

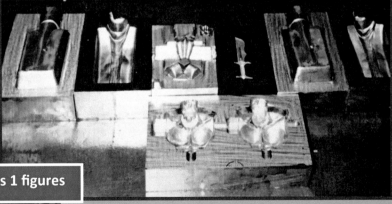

Tooling for the Wetworks Series 1 figures

35

Spawn playing card deck

Trading cards were a big part of Spawn in the early years. Stabur / Caliber did the first prototype card that was released at Toy Fair 1994. However, Todd decided to have Wildstorm Productions produce the first set of Spawn Cards based on the comic book in an oversized format.

Future card editions included the Spawn Movie Cards based on the feature film, Spawn the Toy Files by Inkworks featuring the action figures and toys, and later a full chromium card set featuring Spawn comic covers and new art from comic veterans. Epoch also put out a card set in Japan.

Fun Fact: Spog #9 was misspelled "The Beeding Heart." Did they forget the L in BLEEDING, or misspell BEATING?

The Spawn "Spogz," a set of 54 colorful "milk cap" pogs released in 1993 from Eclipse, was one of the first licensed products to carry the Spawn brand. A second set of 72 pogs was put out by Canada Games in 1997 and was one of the last series of Pogs manufactured before the fad started to fade out.

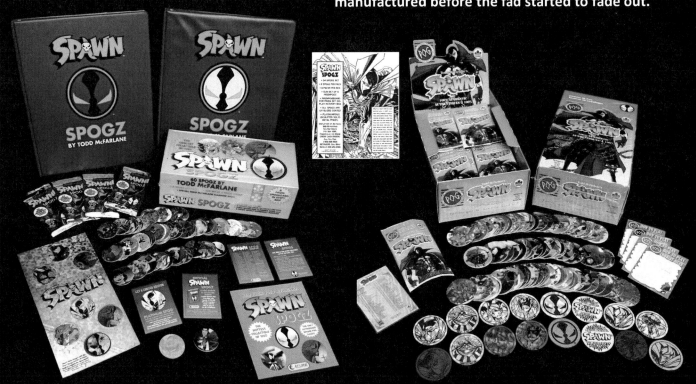

1996 TOY FAIR SHOWROOM

Todd wanted to increase our impact to the buyers in 1996. In addition to three Spawn action figure series and our first 13" Spawn action figures, we expanded the line to include our first non-Spawn action figure series, Total Chaos (created by Todd). Wetworks also carried over into '96 with its second series of figures.

Our 1996 New York Toy Fair showroom featured full size character mannequins for the first time and we increased the level of detail in our themed displays.

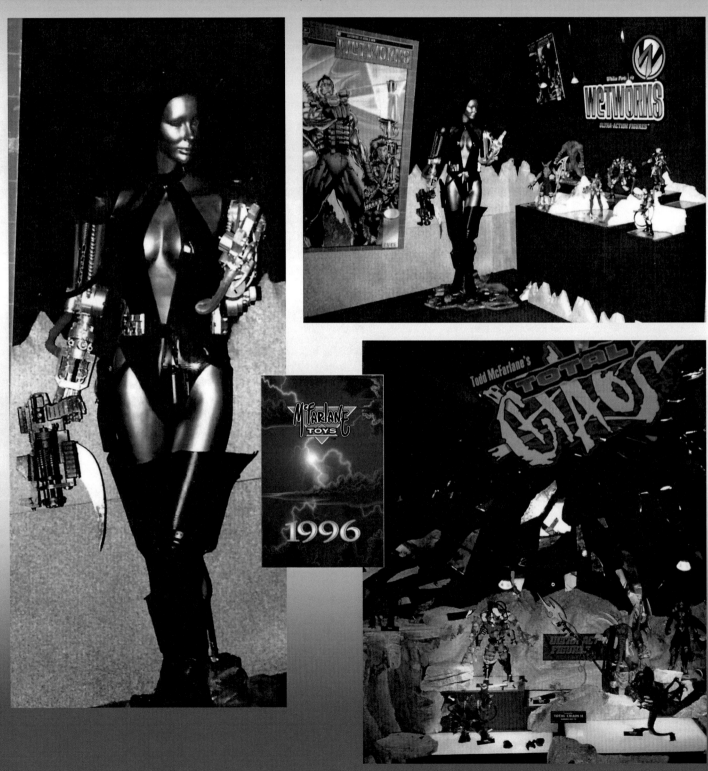

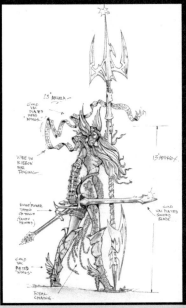

13" Angela Concept Art

At the start of TMP Toys, Todd said that I should stay away from all creative decisions and concentrate on the business. Not being a creative person, I agreed 100% with Todd. A few years later, Tony, Ed, or Bill said they had to get approval for the Gore figure in the Total Chaos series. But Todd was on a rare vacation (or somewhere) and wouldn't be around for a week. What did I think of the sculpt and the huge parrot? The parrot was beautiful and half the size of Gore. I approved it for the run. I just knew it would be a popular toy. When Todd returned, he was furious. He said the toy wouldn't sell. He wanted the parrot to be bigger than Gore. I argued that the toy would sell, as I was convinced it was a great toy. Well... Todd was right, the toy was one of our slower sellers. I never considered making a creative decision again.

COMIC & TOY CONVENTIONS

BARCELONA SPAIN

McFarlane Toys presented at a number of comic conventions throughout the years. From large displays at San Diego Comic Con to small booths in Barcelona, Spain, & Angulema, France. We promoted Spawn everywhere we could reach an audience. In 1996 we set up a booth at Motor City Con. We had a few Malebolgia action figures that we were selling for $60 each. After thinking about it for awhile, a young boy about 12 years old purchased one and then promptly sat on the floor in front of the booth, ripped it out of the package and started playing with it. I gave him his $60 back. It was nice to see someone play with a toy for a change.

ANGULEMA, FRANCE

41

HONG KONG

Hong Kong is an exciting city to visit. A highpoint for Tony Billotto and Bill Martin was their visit during the changeover from British rule to China rule on June 30th, 1997. It was very exciting to be present for the Hong Kong change-over.

We watched the fireworks from the roof of the Royal Garden, along with Jean Claude Van Damme, Rob Schneider, and Paul Sorvino. My son and future wife were there as well. At midnight every street was shut down to traffic for about an hour. It seemed quietly eerie and dreamlike when millions of people came out to just walk around in the streets with no cars. The other eerie thing was watching on TV the columns of Chinese Red Army troops approach Hong Kong. Being in Hong Kong during the Christmas season was also a highlight.

-Tony B.

One of the TMP favorite hangouts was the Empire Tailor Shop next to the hotel and below our office. Every time someone came to Hong Kong, they always stopped in to visit the shop owners and occasionally had a shirt or a suit made. It became well-known and even executives from other companies and friends who traveled there all made the visit to Empire. We would find their business cards taped to the counter whenever we'd visit.

Tony gets a suit made at Empire Tailors.

VIETNAM

In 1996 we visited factories in Vietnam for a few days, exploring the possibility of utilizing other countries as back up sourcing for toy product manufacturing. Primarily we were in the Ho Chi Minh City area of Vietnam. We also visited the Chu Chi Tunnels and the former American Embassy, where during the Vietnam War the last helicopter flights removed US citizens and army personal from Vietnam. It was a very enjoyable, yet different cultural experience. In the end, we never had to manufacture outside of China.

Gretchen Burke, Bob Juranich, Paul Burke, Victor Wong, Pat Carron, Frankie Yeh, Bill Martin and Alan Chan

Temple Dragon

Ho Chi Minh City

Vietnam Temple

V29 Embassy Helicopter

MEETING KISS

While we were designing figures of KISS, some of us from the NJ office had the opportunity to meet the entire band. Eric Treadway, Derrick Miller, my son, and I went out to the Nassau Coliseum to see their concert and to get approvals on our two-up prototypes of the KISS figures. Todd and Wanda also came out to the concert and met us with free tickets at the coliseum.

We waited in a green room for the concert to begin. I went out to the auditorium where thousands of fans were standing and pumping their fists in the air while a single bass drum pounded out a rhythm. I went back into the green room and said, "Hey Todd, you have to see this." He and I went out to watch the fans. Todd was a little stunned. After the concert we met with the band.

My son had brought along an electric guitar, one he restored after finding it at the dump on Martha's Vineyard. The entire band signed his guitar and approved the sculptures we had brought. Shannon Tweed was also present. She wanted us to make blank white KISS figures packed with jars of paint, so that the consumers could decorate their own figures. It was fun watching Todd trying to be diplomatic when that idea was pitched by Shannon.

OCEAN FREIGHT

In early 1996 Bill Martin and I met with our insurance agent to update and renew our insurance policies for TMP. The agent Kevin Sweet brought up "ocean freight" insurance. If a container ship gets into trouble with bad weather or rough seas, they can and sometimes do throw containers off of the ships into the ocean. It's rare, but it does happen. Maritime laws allow this and the freight companies are not responsible for reimbursement for these containers. The shipper simply loses his inventory, only being reimbursed if they had ocean freight insurance.

Bill and I dreaded getting this insurance but it was mandated by our bank. The odds were slim anything would happen and the policy was expensive. Yet to lose a shipment would be very expensive and hurt us during the early years. Six months later, the Hyundai "Minnow" carrying a shipment of McFarlane Toys lost power in the North Pacific about 300 miles off the coast. Then a typhoon came in and the Coast Guard evacuated the ship. Before the crew left, they threw all of the containers overboard. We collected on the insurance policy. Odds of it happening twice within a few years were highly unlikely, so we thought about cancelling the policy. Who knows? One day explorers may find a few sunken containers of our early toys.

1997 SHOWROOM

We pushed the envelope with our displays in the small amount of space we had in New York. Even though we increased space every year, we were out growing it in terms of the number of toy lines as well as by the complexities of our displays.

In 1997, we had four life-size figures of the band KISS in one area promoting the KISS action figures, the new Manga Spawn series, the new McFarlane Monsters series, two additional Spawn lines, and Spawn the Movie series of action figures.

The display themes were getting more complex and detailed. The floor traffic for the showroom was intense. People waited up to fifteen minutes for the rooms to clear before they could enter the display area.

1997 SHOWROOM

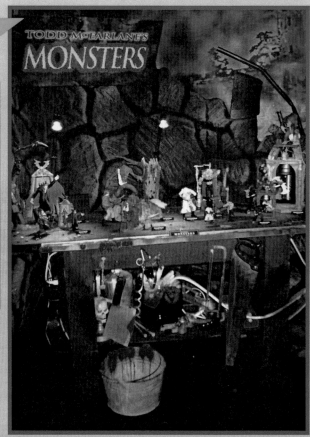

McFARLANE TOYS

Spawn · Total Chaos · KISS · Monsters

1997 the year of SPAWN — PROMOTIONAL VIDEO

McFARLANE TOYS 1997 · Spawn · Total Chaos · Monsters · SPAWN THE MOVIE

Todd McFarlane's MONSTERS

LEGENDARY MONSTERS YOU GREW UP WITH!

DRACULA · WEREWOLF · FRANKENSTEIN · HUNCHBACK

Maintaining the high standard of quality, design, and collectibility that we've become known for, our April line comes straight from the pages of some of the greatest works of literature - 4 classic Monsters that you grew up with!

Each set comes with TWO figures and enough accessories to build your own horror dioramas.

With numerous pieces to each set, the playability goes on and on!

First launched in September 1996, Total Chaos was met with great enthusiasm and acclaim from retailers and consumers alike.

In August, the excitement is sure to continue as the second series of this unique line hits toy shelves.

Total Chaos is our own in-house line. Each highly detailed figure comes exclusively from the imagination and creativity of Todd McFarlane himself.

TOTAL CHAOS

McFarlane Toys
- After only 3 years, McFarlane Toys ranks in the top 10 of action figure manufacturers for units sold
- In 1995, McFarlane Toys experienced the largest industry growth (Source: TRSTS reports)
- Distributed to 15 different countries
- Sold over 10 million units to date

1996 AWARDS/HONORS WON BY McFARLANE TOYS
- Favorite Toy Line - *Spawn* - Wizard Fan Awards
- Hottest Villain of 1996 - Malebolgia - White's Guide to Collecting Figures
- Best Action Figure to Scare Your Pants Off - Sansker - White's Guide to Collecting Figures
- Best Sculpted Figure for 1996 - Vertebreaker - Panged Toy Network
- Top 10 Action Figures for 1996 - #7, Sansker - Wizard
- Best Female Sculpting Award - Blood Queen - White's Guide to Collecting Figures

McFARLANE TOYS

Advertising Campaign
- New Line Cinema national television advertising campaign - April through August
- HBO national television advertising campaign - January through July
- McFarlane Toys network, cable, and spot television advertising campaign - Summer '97 - Timed to increase exposures for continued Spawn recognition
- New Line Cinema national print advertising campaign - April through August
- HBO national print advertising campaign - April through July
- McFarlane Toys national print advertising and Curse of the Spawn comic books
- McFarlane Toys print advertising in both Spawn and Curse of the Spawn comic books - Every month per comic, each reaching over 180,000 readers
- McFarlane Toys national print advertising - expansion into leading music magazines for KISS launch - Summer '97
- McFarlane Toys national print advertising - expansion into children's/youth magazines for Spawn: The Movie line - Summer and fall/winter '97
- McFarlane Toys national print advertising - expansion into entertainment magazines for Spawn: The Movie line - August/September - Timed to increase exposures for continued Spawn name recognition

1997: The Year of Spawn!
Promotion Schedule
- Numerous cross-promotions with New Line Cinema, KISS, HBO, and Sony
- CNN feature on Todd McFarlane to air in the spring
- Access Hollywood piece on Film
- Nationwide Spawn and McFarlane Toys promotions tour (including Spawn with New Line Cinema, Sony, Toy Fairs, along with possible music and movie industry-based promotions)
- Nationwide promotional launch for each McFarlane Toys line
- Premiere Magazine focus on Spawn: The Movie
- L.A. Times Calendar - Cover feature on Spawn and Todd McFarlane
- Entertainment Weekly piece on the phenomenon of Spawn
- Future pieces scheduled for E! Entertainment Television, Hollywood's Greatest Stunts, Movie Magic, Cinefex, American Cinematographer, Entertainment Tonight, BPI, Sci-Fi, Vortex, Boston Globe, Icon, Wall Street Journal, Metal Edge, Spin, Rolling Stone, Interview Magazine and many more!

"McFarlane Toys welcomes

"1997 marks our biggest and most diversified year.

thank you for your continued support."

McFarlane Monsters

In early 1996, toy designers Ed and Tony approached me about designing one of the first non-comic book lines of toys, McFarlane's Monsters. They wanted me to speak to Todd about creating the line, which would include traditional monsters like Frankenstein, Hunchback, etc., but it had to be different in some way. Todd, Ed and Tony created a series of six monsters. Each figure included an individual diorama playset. These dioramas were designed to attach to each other to form a mini playset.

One little known aspect of McFarlane's Monsters is that a limited amount of the Hunchback figures were produced and distributed with an alternate head that featured the likeness of Jim Preziosi, one of the design team members. This started a trend with the design team of sculpting heads with the likenesses of McFarlane designers and producing a limited number of these toys that were sold through regular retail channels. These are true collectibles.

Includes Igor figure, lab table, extra Frankenstein head, lab tools and equipment.

Includes a woodsman, fence, and open-up tree for hiding woodsman.

Includes Executioner figure with battle ax, swinging bell, and a working catapult.

Set has Dracula in human form and bat form. Also includes coffin and transforming crypt action.

SPECIAL / CUSTOM TOYS

Working in a toy company had its opportunities for creating fun.

The toy design team occasionally used themselves and others as models for action figures and sculpted heads of characters with their likeness. A few were produced as the full manufacturing run and some had a limited run.

The McFarlane Monster series has Jim Preziosi as the Hunchback and the "crying head" as the chase figure in the Hunchback playset, Eric Treadaway as Dr. Frankenstein, and Terry "Spanky" Rodgers as the diver in the Creature from the Black Lagoon playset. Steve Hamady was the model for the Steve "The Victim" figure in the Werewolf playset. Also, Steve was the voice for the Marv action figure... "Is that all you got? You pansies!" The Goddess was modeled after Kathy Faline, Billy Mancuso is the Knight (Dragon Blade) from Total Chaos series 1, Eric "Cornboy" Mayse is the Cornboy figure from Total Chaos 2, and Todd was the model for the "Todd the Bum" figure in the Spawn movie set of toys. Who knows what other ones are out there.

McFarlane's Monsters Series 1
Hunchback Variant

McFarlane's Monsters Series 2
Dr. Frankenstein

McFarlane's Monsters Series 2
Sea Creature Diver

McFarlane's Monsters series 1
Werewolf Hunter "Victim"

Manga Spawn series 9
The Goddess

Total Chaos series 1
Dragon Blade

Total Chaos series 2
Cornboy

Spawn Movie Alley Playset
Todd the Bum

Custom toys were created by Chet Jacques and others as joke suggestions for toy production. Malebolgia and Violator were favorites to modify for scenes and dress up in Barbie clothes.

One of our favorites is Happy Meal Todd. Mattel had TMP change the name of Todd Toys to McFarlane Toys. Mattel said people were confused with our Todd Toys and their Happy Meal Todd character and requested we change the company name, as they owned the Todd trademark. We changed the name and then made our own version of Happy Meal Todd for fun.

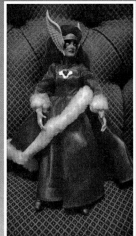

Pink Violator Chopper with crash test helmet Malebolgia.

Happy Meal Todd in packaging.

Dress up Angela and Santa Zeus

Malebolgia Mobile.

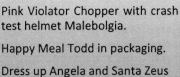

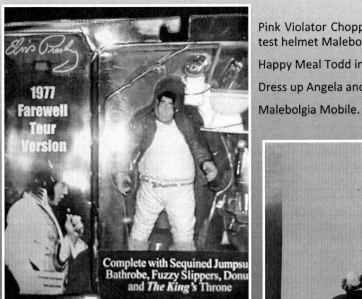

Farewell Tour Elvis: Complete with sequined jumpsuit, bathrobe, fuzzy slipper, donut, and "the King's Throne" toilet

King Conan on porcelain throne diorama

RETAILER EXCLUSIVES

In early 1995 I decided to go with our VP of Sales Bob LoMonaco on a sales call to see Kerry McVay, the toy buyer at K-Mart. K-Mart was a Detroit based business and a good account for TMP. We wanted them to become a major account for TMP.

During the meeting Kerry complained he was getting his toys after Walmart, Toys R Us, etc. and wanted to know how he could get the toys faster and draw in the initial collector customers. He had just received a large re-order of toys, so I told him to not open the cases. I would replace them with a new re-paint line that was landing in Seattle the next day and I would swap them out. He would be the first with the re-painted toys. He was thrilled and promised to double our SKU's (pegs) for Christmas.

Bob and I talked briefly and we decided to offer K-Mart a Medieval Spawn and Malebolgia 2-pack retailer exclusive. K-Mart had never received an exclusive from us in the past and this was one of the best ones we could think of offering. They received 20,000 specials and sold out of them within one week.

The success led us to do another 2-pack of Violator and Commando Spawn for Target.

The trend caught on as later exclusives included gold repaints of our series one figures for KB Toys, as well as exclusives for Hills, Toys R Us, and other toy retailers.

SPAWN MOVIE & PROMOTION

TMP was a collaboration of different businesses directed by Todd. Each business unit fed off of the others. While McFarlane Toys made great action figures, it was the cross promotion from the comic books, movies, sound recordings, and licenses that generated awareness of Spawn and TMP products.

One of the highlights in 1997 was the release of Spawn the Movie and its soundtrack album that generated consumer awareness to millions of people worldwide.

SPAWN MOVIE FIGURES

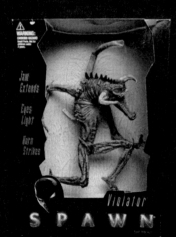

SPAWN MOVIE SOUNDTRACK

Our attitude of "controlling our destiny" extended from making Spawn the movie to producing the Spawn movie soundtrack. Terry Fitzgerald, the President of Todd McFarlane Entertainment, worked with Al Masocco of Sony Entertainment to create a unique soundtrack. They teamed up with some of the leading music groups on individual songs, creating one of the best movie soundtracks of all time. The Spawn movie soundtrack went Platinum within 6 months of release and sold over 3 million copies worldwide.

This established Todd McFarlane Entertainment in the music industry. The company produced Grammy Award winning music videos and received ten MTV Music Video nominations, a record at the time.

Todd McFarlane Entertainment went on to create and produce the Spawn HBO Series, winning two Emmys for Best Animated Program in 1998 and 1999.

JAPAN

In 1996, we decided to expand internationally. The first country we decided to develop was Japan. First, we needed to get Spawn published in Japan to create a reading audience. One of our Chinese associates, Charles Ip, suggested that I join a Japanese CEO network to ensure we found the right publisher to affiliate with and he would arrange it.

I met with twelve CEO's from Japan's leading companies. A driver took me to six meetings a day for two days where I was briefly introduced to each CEO in a five minute meeting. The final meeting was with Media Works, our potential publisher.

This meeting consisted of ten people, and I was asked numerous business and personal questions for a few hours. I mentioned where I lived and the translator asked me how far I lived from the fire station. I answered 1/8th of a mile, and then wondering, asked him how he knew I lived by a fire station. He had graduated from University of Michigan and lived in the area during that time he went to college. We signed them as our publisher and decided to create the Manga Spawn toy line to help promote the comic book in Japan.

MANGA SPAWN

We signed a sub-publishing agreement with Media Works, a leading Japanese publisher, to publish the Spawn comics in Japan. We decided to create the Manga Spawn action figure lines to attract the Japanese consumers and give attention to the Spawn comic book.

Manga Spawn became one of our most popular toy series both in the US and Japan. It propelled the Spawn comic book to the #1 bestselling US comic book in Japan and led the way to numerous license and entertainment ventures for a number of years.

Manga Ninja Spawn
Design Sketch

Manga Curse
Design Sketch

Manga Clown
Design Sketch

JAPAN TOY FAIR

Peter Irwin with Angela model at Tokyo Toy Fair

Paul Burke, Angela, and Terry Fitzgerald

Angela draws a crowd at the Tokyo Toy Fair.

Spawn's entry into the Japanese market was massive. The Spawn comic book jumped to the number #1 US comic book immediately and the fans clamored for more. Rick Privman, Yumiko Miyano and Media Works pushed the brand to new heights with strategic licenses and the creation of a Manga Spawn comic book to appease the fans. When Manga Spawn and the other McFarlane Toys action figures hit the market in 1997 at Japan Toy Fair, the reception and sales were astonishing. The success in Japan led to numerous specialty retailers selling complete lines of Spawn merchandise and caused company growth throughout Southeast Asia.

JAPAN LICENSING

We added Rick Privman and Yumiko Miyano of Japan Exchange Association (JEA) to the Japan team in 1997. Rick and Yumiko worked with Terry Fitzgerald, who was the head of licensing for all of Todd's companies, arranging licenses and coordinating promotion and business activities.

Japan was such a fanatical market, they had their own collector club with special merchandise. Many licensing deals were signed providing the rabid fans with Spawn licensed merchandise such as apparel, watches, lighters, jewelry, puzzles, cell phone accessories, and vinyl toys.

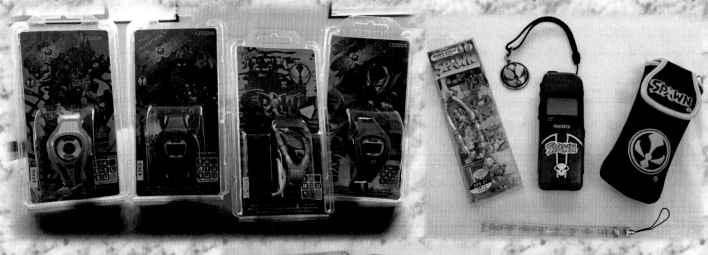

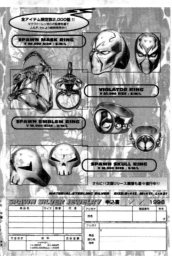

VAN TOURS & SPAWN TRUCKS

While the Spawn Mobile and the Crime Mobile toured conventions and auto shows around North America, TMP also had custom vans and trucks that visited other events around the states. The company initially had a custom painted '95 Chevy cube van for convention use and then a 26' Freightliner custom painted for Midwest deliveries. Both trucks were traveling billboards that generated more waving, honking and truck stop conversations than we could have imagined.

Then TMP launched its Spawn custom van tours. Each van was equipped at the TMP warehouse with a large screen television, stereo system, and custom interior. The electronics work was done mainly by Bob LoMonaco, our VP of Sales who was quite skilled at van customization.

Bob LoMonaco & Paul Burke prepare the van for touring.

The vans toured the country stopping at any event that drew a crowd. They toured with the Oz Fest tour, the Lollapalooza tour, attended national sporting events (MLB games), movie premiers, and made random, un-planned store appearances at comic shops and mass retailers as they traveled the country.

At each stop the van team would play promotion videos featuring the various company entertainment projects, comic books, and products. Then they would give away comic books, buttons, pins, shirts, hats, and an occasional Spawn jacket.

Needless to say, the van tours were very popular.

Dave Eisenhardt with the Spawn movie van

I may not have ever worked for TMP or McFarlane Toys, but they greatly influenced my youth and even adulthood to this day.

I was 15 when Image Comics came along, and with it, Spawn. I had never really collected anything up to that point. However, I collected all the Image books I could get my hands on, and something about the green logo of Spawn sunk its hooks in me deep. At that time, I didn't collect toys. A few years later McFarlane Toys was formed and I grabbed a full case of Series 1 at the store. From then on, collecting was in my blood. Then came the Spawn.com message boards where I could interact with other fans. There was a whole other world that formed with the fans on the message boards, and a lot of that was due to the people at Mcfarlane Toys. They helped nurture that community by interacting with us and letting us see behind the curtain a bit. I made life-long friends with many of the people I met through those boards. There was nothing like it, and probably never will be again.

Over the years I became friends with one of the moderators, Joe Ferstl, through those message boards. He's always been an advocate for me and the dedicated nature of my Spawn collection. If I had a hard time tracking something down, he would try and help me out as best he could by checking with others in the office, sending me something he had, or just generally keeping me in the loop of upcoming releases.

One year I took a trip out to Phoenix to see him and we were talking over lunch about stuff. I asked him how he came to work at Mcfarlane Toys. He told me he started off with the company doing the Spawn van tours, traveling around to different events around 1997. I then relayed a story about sitting outside an ice cream shop many years ago, and seeing a Spawn van drive past me. I immediately ran after it. I didn't know what the van was for or why it was in my small town, but I had to find out. I caught up with the van and started talking with the guys that were driving it. They said they were in town for Oz Fest. I told them about my obsession with Spawn and my ever growing collection. Then one guy walked to the back of the van and pulled out a bagged Manga Overtkill figure and gave it to me. I still have it to this day.

As it turns out, I am 99% sure the guy that gave me the figure was Joe F. Based on what I told him and his time frame and description of himself at the time we are pretty sure it was him, probably a good 5 years before I met him on the message boards where he took note of my collection.

- Steve Gouge aka Punkg42

COLLECTOR'S CLUBS

Chet Jacques, one of the McFarlane Toys team, managed the McFarlane Collectors Club and arranged convention promotion. Chet was our in-house expert on what toys we had produced and how the collectors and fans reacted to them. Chet is also known for the unique versions of our toys and customs he created to fit special occasions.

The club started with the Red Violator in 1995 as a way to move excess inventory. This was done domestically. For fans who sent in 3 proofs of purchase UPC's (original not copies) we sent a free red Violator. The thought was to generate sales of inventory at store levels where we had offered markdown credit. We were finding out that our figures were huge in the collector's market. Discounted sales would allow the purchaser the opportunity to buy 3 figures cheap, open them to get the proof of purchase, and mail away for the free Violator.

Chet had been answering questions about various figures on a USENET group for about a year. This was before the Spawn website was up and thriving. Chet convinced Todd that we could do well with selling direct to the public on certain toys and ran a contest: "Send me your name and address if you read this group, and you could win an official two-up figure of one of our toys." We had a few sitting in our Livonia office after they had been approved. Within two weeks, he had about 1,000 names. Combining the rebate responses and Chet's collector list, the Collectors Club got rolling.

The Collector Club released the Necroplasm Spawn, Red Angela, Heavenly Fire Angela, Bag of Dragons, Bag of Demons, Bag of Iszs, Collector's Display Cases, Bag of Stands, Wanda, Cogliostro, and Jason Wynn figures exclusive to the club, as well as many other non-exclusive action figures over the years.

Fun Fact: Jason Wynn's "Confidential Files"
are just copied pages of a dictionary.

The first exclusives had to be a good ones, worth shelling out a few dollars for, but not costing much in production due to the limited run we were making. I took one of the competitor toys on my desk, a Mucus Tick figure, cut the antennae off, and fitted it with a Spawn cape and belt. They were the same size, and made a great example of what Necroplasm Spawn would look like. - Chet J.

Within a few months the club had thousands of members, and approximately 40% were members from Japan. So we created a second club, the McFarlane Toys Japan Collector Club which offered gold and silver Spawns and an assortment of other Spawn toys and products. The Japanese club was started as a way to avoid the high shipping costs internationally. However, most Japanese collectors joined both clubs to get all the exclusive toys and merchandise.

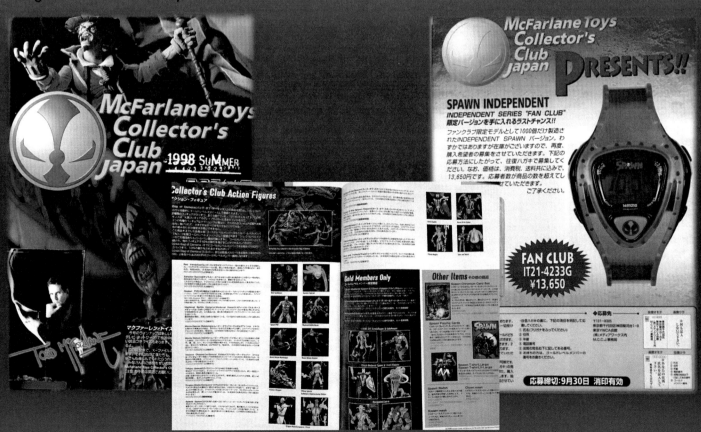

1998 SHOWROOM

1997 was our last year in Al Gilly's New York showroom. Once we started producing life-size figures to dramatize our action figure lines, we knew we had to move to our own showroom.

In the summer of 1997, the company leased 5,000 square feet of office space in the high-demand Lower Midtown Manhattan, in the toy district, for its new McFarlane Toys showroom. The space sat empty until January, 1998. Then the fun began.

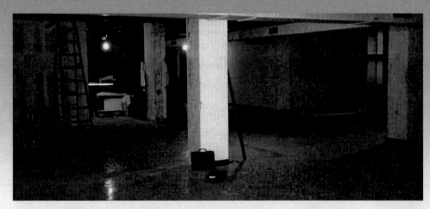

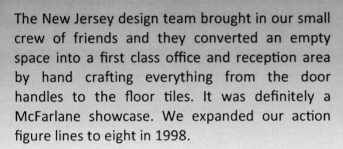

The New Jersey design team brought in our small crew of friends and they converted an empty space into a first class office and reception area by hand crafting everything from the door handles to the floor tiles. It was definitely a McFarlane showcase. We expanded our action figure lines to eight in 1998.

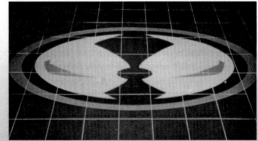

The design team converted the back area of the showroom into a series of display rooms, each room a highly detailed environment specific to the toy line featured in the room. The displays featured elaborate electronics, fog machines, sound recordings, special models, and life-size figures. The showroom became an industry must-see by all the buyers and toy executives.

All of our display rooms were modeled after the appropriate toy line. Our Movie Maniacs display with a life size figure of Freddy Krueger coming through a door was a huge hit with the buyers and set the tone for the future.

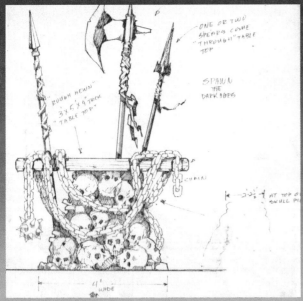

Design for Dark Ages Spawn showroom display table

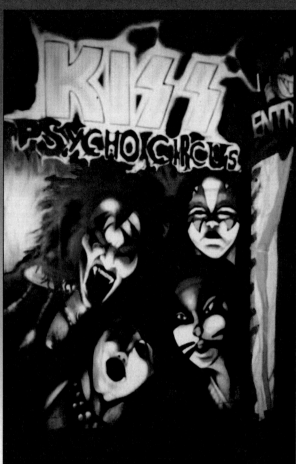

One of the challenges we had with the X-Files line was how to deal with 20th Century Fox's very tight restrictions and requirements. (at least with McFarlane Toys.) Fox told us that they did not want us to display the alien figure at Toy Fair. They wanted the reveal of their alien to be a big surprise for the series' fans, because it had never been shown in the TV series. Of course, the main reason for procuring the X-Files movie license was to capitalize on the hoped-for success of the upcoming film. We certainly understood that Fox wanted to build up the hype around the world in finally getting the chance to see their alien for the first time. We asked Fox for permission to at least show the alien to the buyers only. The buyers had to see what they would be buying. After much wrangling, they agreed to let us do so. We built a special display using two-way mirrored mylar film that lined a large clear Plexiglas tube. The tube was lighted from within. The alien figure was displayed inside the clear tube. When the light was turned off, the figure could not be seen. When the light was on the buyers could view the alien clearly. We only turned the light on for the buyers, not for the press or any other toy fair attendees. 20th Century Fox still came to the showroom and had a team of Fox people cut all of the images of the X-Files alien toys out of our catalogs.

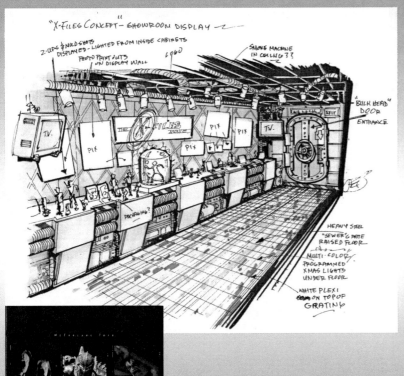

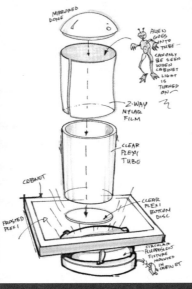

McFARLANE PEOPLE

Bob McFarlane

Bob McFarlane, Todd's father, had retired a few months before the start of McFarlane Toys and was a flawless Spawn promoter. Everyone loved Bob, his personality and positive attitude were a plus to the organization and all of the employees. We never gave Bob a plan or schedule. He just traveled. Bob toured retailers, conventions, anywhere, just stopping in to promote Spawn and all the publications and products. Bob was everywhere, including Hong Kong sporadically to spread his goodwill. Bob, a professional harmonica player, occasionally played harmonica with a Pilipino cowboy band in Hong Kong. (Above Left & Right)

Victor Wong and Bill Martin

Terry Fitzgerald and Clive Barker

Bill Martin and Paul Burke at Coconut Restaurant

Beau Smith and Julia Simmons

McFarlane Toys was a great toy company. It was a great experience bringing the highest quality products and action figures to market that we could possibly produce. The company also taught the TMP team how to grow as a business from a simple startup to a successful international company working in many industries. During this adventure we experienced many different cultures and gained international business experience beyond our imagination. The key people at McFarlane Toys traveled hundreds of thousands of miles every year around the world. This was only possible with understanding spouses, families and all of the TMP team members everywhere. The company was fortunate to be able to have them travel with us occasionally on our adventures.

Bobby and Peter Cheng

Governor Vieira in black shirt / sunglasses)

In November of 1996, Bill Martin, Pat Carron, Mike, Kovalcheck, Peter Yeh and I went to Macau to see the Macau Grand Prix. The trip was unplanned, just something to do on a Sunday. So when we got there, we purchased the only available "standing room only" tickets. The grandstands were jammed with people. Bill and Peter went in one direction looking for a seat, and Pat and I went another direction. Pat wandered off and came back 20 minutes later and said he had us seats. Pat and I went to the front row at the starting line and security guards let us into the first row to sit with Governor Vieira from Portugal to watch the race. All Pat would tell me was that the Governor thought he knew us and we got the best seats in the house.

Tina Daniels and Bill Martin

Victor Wong

Pat Carron somewhere in the world

Peter Irwin at Nurnberg Toy Fair

Paul Burke at Soul Train Café Tokyo

Gretchen Burke

Steven Spielberg reviewing Jaws sculpture

73

TMP ENTERTAINMENT

From 1997 on, Todd and Terry Fitzgerald created artwork for album covers and directed and/or produced music videos for a number of the top music groups in the world: Pearl Jam, Korn, Disturbed, Marilyn Manson, Swollen Members, and more. Their efforts resulted winning two Emmys for Best Animated Series for the HBO Spawn animation, two Grammy nominations and one win for Best Music Video for Korn's Freak on a Leash. They also received a record ten MTV Music Video Awards nominations with two wins, also for the Korn video. In Canada they took home four nominations and one win for the Swollen Member's video at the Much Music Video Awards. The band Disturbed even used McFarlane artwork to wrap their promotional funny car.

PEARL JAM
Animation Cel from the "DO THE EVOLUTION" Music Video
DIRECTED BY TODD McFARLANE

Terry Fitzgerald on MTV Japan

Terry Fitzgerald with Howard Stern

SPEC RACING / FORD NASCAR

The Ford Motor Company recognized the popularity and appeal of Spawn to young people and approached TMP to sponsor and assist the Los Angeles Police Department with its "Safety Awareness" program for school children. The LAPD was touring schools with a custom racing Ford Bronco vehicle that they ran in all of the professional off-road races. The police officers spoke to the kids about achieving life goals, having fun, and being safe. Their association with TMP brought in a whole new level of being cool and achieving goals. TMP provided the LAPD with comic books, stickers, and tattoos to give out at the events. Ford and the LAPD invited us as their guest to attend the Mint 400 race in Las Vegas. Julia Simmons and I attended the race and solidified a relationship that extended to NASCAR. Over the next few years, Ford Motor Company provided us with free pickup trucks to use in exchange for mileage data and promotion visibility. I made a personal investment into a SPEC racer to be driven by Andy Slankard to utilize the Ford trucks and generate publicity for Ford and TMP. As our relationship grew, Ford wanted to replace two of their NASCAR race cars with a Spawn and Violator imaged cars. Ford invited me to a few NASCAR races as their guest for a behind-the-scenes education and it was an unforgettable on-track experience for me. The Ford Motor Company presented TMP with a lucrative offer for the NASCAR car naming rights, but it was offered at a time when we just could not accept it.

During my time with McFarlane Toys, most especially while working in their showroom at the International Toy Fair in NYC, I had some of my most memorable experiences, both professionally and personally. Throughout my 40-year career working as an artist, never have I had so many laughs and learned so much. (Thanks Tony!)

Working with such a great group of dynamic people, some of whom I still have dear friendships today, I cherish the memories of those good ol' days! There was such a dynamic cast of characters on our team of creatives. In addition to all the laughs, we worked very long hours and spent a lot of time together. With so many incidents to choose from, the funniest moment was, by far, when our pal Dan 'the Man' Marchese had a bizarre 'interaction' with a plasma ball that was installed in one of our environments. I do believe our fearless team leader, Anthony Billotto, can provide a proper account of that hilarious incident.

My most satisfying moment was when our collective effort was first credited and showcased by Wizard Magazine as being an "award-winning" showroom at Toy Fair. This was the start of a successive winning streak for our TMP showroom year in, and year out. It was particularly gratifying for me to play a role on such a winning team, considering we were competing with the extravagant showrooms of the major toy companies at that time. It was hard to go up against Hasbro, Mattel, etc. Their artisans were working with significantly deeper budgets. Every year, most companies gutted their showrooms, recycled what they could and trashed the rest. So the street artist in me decided to lead a charge and dumpster dive through their dumpsters. We had discovered that they discarded all sorts of props and materials, mostly undamaged and ready to be transmuted into creative materials, fueling our artistic team to craft some dazzling sets and environments, award-winning, if I may. It was so much sweeter that we gave the toy majors a run for their money, considering the odds, and with their own trash no less!

I miss those great times with those cherished friends. Rest in peace to our friends Ken 'Ken Zen' Hoare and James 'Child' Byrne Jr.

Best,
Carmelo 'Snow' Sigona

Look for more of Carmelo's graffiti artwork throughout the McFarlane Toys showroom displays.

AUSTIN POWERS

METAL GEAR

TECHNO SPAWN

SPAWN
THE DARK AGES

CURSE OF THE
SPAWN

KISS
PSYCHO CIRCUS

The Beatles
Yellow Submarine

OZZY OSBOURNE

MOVIE MANIACS

TIM BURTON'S
Sleepy Hollow

2.50 USA 4.00 CAN
www.mcfarlane.com

The Scarlet Edge

SPAWN
THE DARK AGES
SERIES 14

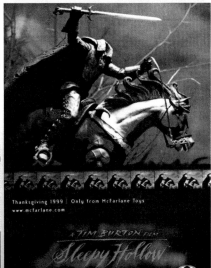

Thanksgiving 1999 | Only from McFarlane Toys
www.mcfarlane.com

A TIM BURTON FILM
Sleepy Hollow

SPAWN: The Black Heart

SPAWN
THE DARK AGES
SERIES 14

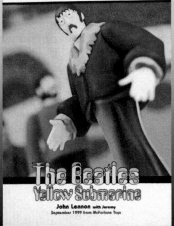

The Beatles
Yellow Submarine

John Lennon with Jeremy
September 1999 from McFarlane Toys

CURSE OF THE
SPAWN

McFARLANE TOYS

TOY FAIR
1999

1999 SHOWROOM

The showroom was a huge attraction in 1999. Todd exhibited his baseball collection of all the record setting home runs between Sammy Sosa and Mark McGuire, including the record #70 homerun baseball.

Todd also made appearances on the Today Show with Matt Lauer and Tom Brokaw for NPR. The baseball collection then went on a MLB stadium tour generating countless interviews and publicity for the upcoming sports action figure lines.

The Spawn series continued with the addition of two new series, the Curse of the Spawn and Techno Spawn. Then Ozzy Osbourne and the Beatles Yellow Submarine joined Kiss as new music orientated action figures. Rounding out the toy lines with Sin City, Movie Maniacs, Austin Powers, Danger Girls, and Metal Gear Solid made 1999 a flagship year.

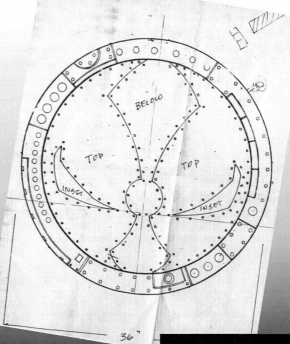

Design drawing for Techno Spawn shield display

TECHNO SPAWN

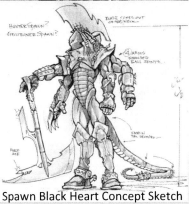

Spawn Black Heart Concept Sketch

1999 was a breakthrough year with twelve action figure series coming out, including Tim Burton's Sleepy Hollow series in later that year corresponding with the film release. The Sleepy Hollow series of action figures brought a lot of one-on-one time with director Tim Burton. Bill Martin and Ed Frank met with Tim on the Sleepy Hollow movie set in England to get approval on the action figure sculptures and fine tune the severed heads that would come packed with the figures. They had a great time in London. The toy business has its advantages at times for sure.

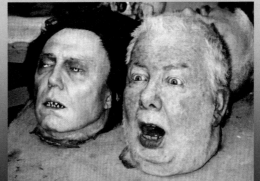

Sleepy Hollow severed head movie props along with their toy counterparts above

JEAN ST. JEAN

When asked what his favorite figures were that he worked on while at McFarlane Toys, Jean St. Jean replied they were Medieval Spawn III, Samurai Spawn, and Edward Scissorhands. To him, Edward Scissorhands really seemed to capture the true essence and frailty of that Johnny Depp character.

He also mentioned that he would meander into the area where Ed and Tony had their drawing boards in order to sneak glimpses of what they were working on. Jean said, "I wanted to see what direction we were going in and then try to angle for which future figure I would like to sculpt."

The Medieval Spawn III figure is an example of how far our figures evolved. Compare this to our first Medieval Spawn entry. Not that the first figures were bad, we just got better and better. By the way, Jean had spent most of his previous professional sculpting years as a top doll sculptor! A couple of years before we hired him, the doll sculpting business where he worked received images from us with a bidding request. Jean saw the images and begged his boss to bid. She did not and Jean sadly went back to sculpting dolls for another year or two. I guess it was fate, because ultimately Jean became one of our stand-out sculptors.

HONG KONG OFFICES

TMP opened a small McFarlane Toys Asia office in 1998 and quickly outgrew the space. We then opened a larger office in 2000. Our principal factory APEX also opened its Hong Kong office in 2000.

Tony Billotto enjoys the view from his desk.

Houston Center Hong Kong office

Victor Wong makes a call.

Peter Cheng, Bobby Cheng, Bill Martin, Victor Wong and Danny To

Bobby Cheng and Bill Martin

2000 proved to be another busy year for the company. Production of over 70 figures spread out over 13 action figure lines. It was also the first year of sports figures with the introduction of the Big League Challenge baseball and NHLPA Hockey action figure lines.

Toy Fair was exciting as usual. The unique displays continued to attract a large contingent of buyers. McFarlane Toys hosted their first International Night at Toy Fair. A cocktail party for all the International buyers was a huge success. Attended by buyers from over 50 countries it was a testament to the vast appeal of McFarlane Toys products.

The Hong Kong office expanded with the addition of two new hires, one offering engineering experience and the other for processing International orders.

The Sales staff moved from the Plymouth office to Tempe, a move that allowed Todd to directly interact on a daily basis with Sales.

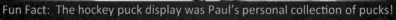
Fun Fact: The hockey puck display was Paul's personal collection of pucks!

The display rooms featured stadium and arena situations, music settings, and our traditional monster displays. Every year the showroom displays got more elaborate than the last. Two of the more interesting and complex lines for 2000 were the Where the Wild Things Are and Sleepy Hollow. Both lines had very interesting action figures.

During the setup of the Spawn Interlink 6 display, Dan was hooking up one of those large static electricity glass balls to a giant free-flying asteroid for our connecting robot figures. There was a flat table area cut into the asteroid to display the robot two-ups. The static ball was to simulate a mysterious power source from which the robots could receive energy. I was working on a display across the aisle from Dan. I glanced over my shoulder to see Dan, standing on his tip toes, leaning over the display about to touch his right eye to the static globe! I'm sure you know that when these globes are touched by one's finger, that one gets shocked. I yelled, "Dan, what are you doing!?" He snapped backwards when his eyeball was shocked by the globe. I ran over to him, not knowing what to expect when I looked at his eye. His eye looked OK but he said it really stung from the shock. I asked him why he did that. He just said that he was curious to see what would happen if he touched his eye to the ball. Who the heck thinks like this?!? I said something like, "OK, Dan, I'm glad you're alright...Now, PLEASE don't do that again." Guess what? Two minutes later I saw him lean over and touch his left eye to the globe! He snapped back, shocked again, and rubbed his eye. I yelled, "What the hell are you doing!?" He answered, saying that if he had damaged his right eye, he wanted to damage the left eye so that they would be"equally balanced!" Unbelievable but true!

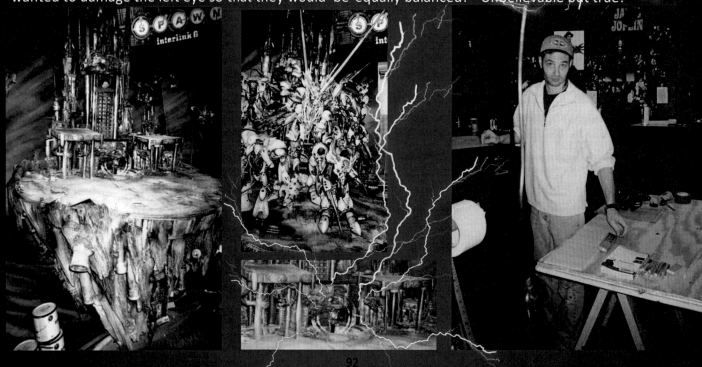

SPAWN 17
CONCEPT
SKETCH

RAT/SKULL BASE

Note: Although prototypes were shown at Toy Fair, the South Park action figures from McFarlane Toys never made it into production.

KING KONG

The tradition of elaborate displays continued until McFarlane left the Manhattan Showroom building.

The success of McFarlane Toys was not solely founded on Todd and the design team's quest to create, manufacture and market unique and highly decorated action figures. The success of McFarlane Toys came from everyone in all of the McFarlane companies.

We made great toy products. Nonetheless, the Spawn comic book boosted awareness of existing characters and introduced new characters for the toy lines. The Spawn Movie, HBO Series, licensing, and publishing created new toy opportunities and brought in consumers worldwide.

We brought Spawn to the people through conventions, van tours, and numerous promotion opportunities. The behind the scene activities were created and carried out by various company individuals working together around the world, promoting the company's efforts and pushing the company to ever increasing heights of success.

Paul Burke, co-founder and co-CEO of TMP International, Inc. (McFarlane Toys). Burke was responsible for the business structure and growth of the company. Alongside Todd, who directed the creative end of the business and related business functions, and together with the McFarlane team of associates, they operated an ever-growing global company.

Bill Martin, President and COO of McFarlane Toys. Martin was responsible for overseeing all aspects of McFarlane Toys from operations, manufacturing, and sales.

Anthony Billotto, Co-President McFarlane Design, Inc. Billotto and Ed Frank became Co-Presidents of McFarlane Design in 1994 to supervise all in-house and outside contract product design and development. They generated concept sketches, figure renderings, control art, sculpted figures, fabricated accessories, created photo sets, designed displays, developed packing, and more. Billotto and Frank worked directly with the overseas factories, which involved price negotiations, scheduling, quality control, sourcing, and finding new factories as needed. Anthony Billotto, Ed Frank, and Bill Martin [TMP President] traveled to Hong Kong/China in an effort to strategically maintain an almost constant ranking presence overseas. The trips helped maintain quality control, keep to the production schedules, and head off any future production problems. They interacted with sales representatives. They also designed and maintained the dynamic New York City showroom.

Rick Privman, the President of JEA. Privman was responsible for coordinating all of Japan's business functions and licensing.

Terence Fitzgerald, foundational employee at the McFarlane companies. Hired fresh out of college, Fitzgerald played an integral role in the formation of Todd McFarlane Productions, the comic book company, McFarlane Toys, and Todd McFarlane Entertainment (the feature film, television, and animation company based in Los Angeles). At TMP, he worked on the production of the Spawn comic book, licensing for third party companies, and video game production. At McFarlane Toys, he acquired licenses from major motion picture studios, music companies, and video game companies. At TME he produced and co-directed animation and music videos for Korn, Pearl Jam, Disturbed, and Swollen Members.

Stephen Gouge, a collector who has an ever-growing collection dedicated to Spawn and McFarlane Toys. A self proclaimed 'Spawn Archivist', he collects anything and everything from the early days and beyond of McFarlane Toys and Image Comics. To his joy, his massive collection finally served a purpose in aiding in the making of this book, a personal dream project.

Acknowledgements

Creating a company like McFarlane Toys is a "once in a lifetime" achievement. We knew we would be successful, no one imagined the success we would achieve. We had a simple aspiration... Make the best action figures possible and control our destiny. The creative direction and vision of Todd McFarlane made this possible.

The commitment and faith of Todd McFarlane and Wanda Kolomyjec to build a company was a trust in the TMP team. We succeeded as a team of people from every McFarlane company. We worked side-by-side coordinating toys, publishing and entertainment to promote and market. We had our successes, we had our disagreements, we learned more in a few short years about global business than any university degree could teach a person. We were proud of what we accomplished playing against the big companies. It was quite the adventure.

None of this would have been possible without all of the McFarlane team associates. Each person had a specific job and each one carried it out to the best of their ability.

We also need to acknowledge our manufacturers, warehousing, agents and sales representatives. Life was simplified by companies like APEX, Norvanco and Irwin Toy, our agents; Lucky Yeh and JEA our sales reps Al Gilly and Associates, Barry Balleci Sales, Smick & Associates, Levin & Schneider, Diverse Marketing, and the Northern Group, and our worldwide sales representatives and distributors, without them the growth would have been much different.

Thank you to everyone for being a part of TMP.

Steve would like to thank all the other collectors that make the world of collecting Spawn fun. Whether it be meet-ups, trading, selling, sharing knowledge, or just through conversations, thank you all for making the message boards and the game of collecting a great place to be.

A special thanks to those that have had a sizeable impact by helping me out acquiring hard to find or unique items, their friendships, and thinking of me and my collection when letting go of items because you know they will have a good home.

Andy Chan (Spawn&Wanda), Trent Claus (Lobstrocity), Victor Farr (Bonedust213), Max Cottica (Irish Spawn), Alan Harding (Aspawnfan), Richard Kisielka (Endquest/ONEYE), John Falk (Juan 2.0).

Made in United States
North Haven, CT
15 April 2022

18301221R00058